THE BRASS RING

Also by Marc Elihu Hofstadter

Poetry:

House of Peace
Visions
Shark's Tooth
Luck
Rising at 5 AM
Memories I've Forgotten
Autumnal
Life Is Its Own Meaning

Prose:

Healing the Split

THE BRASS RING

by Marc Elihu Hofstadter

Walnut Creek, California, 2020

Front cover photograph by Laura Hofstadter

Back cover author photo by Patricia Teschner

ISBN: 9798680651797

Printed in the United States of America

ACKNOWLEDGMENTS

Two friends contributed mightily to both the editing and publication of this book: Donald Sackheim and Patricia Teschner.

TABLE OF CONTENTS

BISEXUAL

ILLNESS

STREAM OF WORDS

REVOLUTION

HOT AND COLD

TROUBADOUR SONG

for David Zurlin

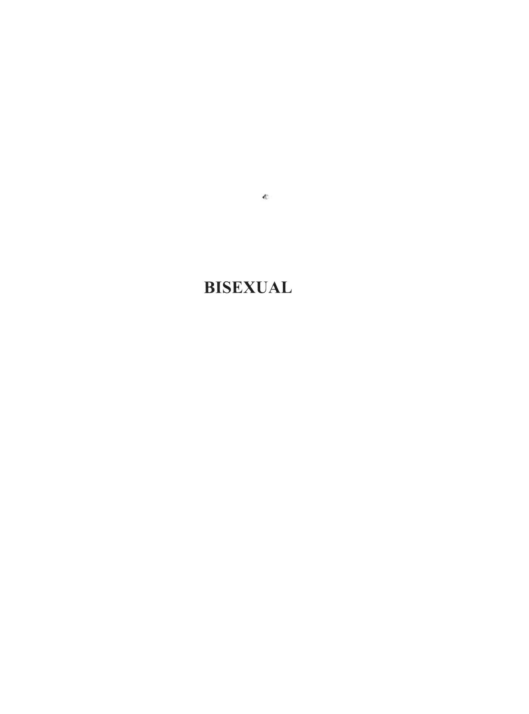

BISEXUAL

I AM BISEXUAL

It's taken a long time.
From age eighteen to age thirty-five
I lived as a straight man.
I had joy in relationships with Ann and Prudence
and was married to the pretty Jill,
knowing at the same time I equally wanted Ron and Tom.
At thirty-five, though, I found my lover Mark,
and that set my way for decades more
of pleasure with Chris and Douglas.
To my surprise, at seventy-four,
I feel neither straight nor gay.
I watch *Klute* and desire Jane Fonda's
breasts. I see a parade
of women entering my tea house
whose curves and hair excite my senses.
I also lust after the muscular Fabrice in
the movie *The Charterhouse of Parma.*
I know myself better than ever,
and like myself as I am.

NEITHER THIS NOR THAT

I don't embrace straight men's culture.
I don't play linebacker,
whistle after women,
cheer for policemen chasing a suspect.
(Not that all straight men do these.)
I don't embrace gay men's culture, either.
I don't engage in campy humor,
enjoy drag queens,
have sex in parks at night.
(Not that all gay men do these.)
I am in between:
I like to play tennis and ping pong,
drink in moderation,
write poetry about a boyfriend
and a girlfriend.
I am neither this nor that.

I AM WHO I AM

When my friend Bob showed me
a girlie magazine, my penis
strained against my belly.
In college I bought *Playboy*
for big breasts and small buns.
When Prudence and I tramped
mountain trails to Silver Lake,
I kept thinking about the space
between her legs.
And yet I've always loved men's
smooth chests, wide shoulders,
hairy thighs, Roman noses.
Although it's been confusing,
I've now given up trying to label myself.
Don't you categorize me, either. I exist.

PEOPLE LABEL ME

"I am large, I contain multitudes!"
I have penis-played in bed with
my buddy Larry at age eight.
I have made out with slim, dark Lyra
in a movie theater at age twelve.
I lost my cherry in a dark green room
with Ann at twenty-two.
I have kissed Prudence madly under the stars
by Thousand Islands Lake at twenty-four.
I have been dominated and fucked
by burly Mark at thirty-five.
What have I been or not been?
Should I fight against my nature?
Who can tell me what I am?

BEING BISEXUAL

I had sex with boys
as a kid, but also
made out with Lyra
in the movie theater.
Was I "queer"?
Had hot sex with Ann
at 23, fell in love
with Prudence at 25,
and married Jill at 30,
but got it on with Mark
at 37, which felt good.
Am I "gay"?
There's no answer,
except that I'm both.

NEITHER

You don't have to be
a straight man
or a gay woman
or a straight woman
to love women
who are compassionate,
sensitive, and
caring.
You don't have to be
a gay man
or a straight woman
to love men
who are strong
and loving.
I love both men and women
and I am neither
straight nor gay.

A LIFE OF PASSION

Be with one,
miss the other.
Hold a cock,
miss a cunt.
Love one,
love both.
I've been two people
all my life, two
at odds with one another.
I've never been at peace,
but have had lots of passion,
always wanting something more,
always in love with some man
or woman.

SEX FIEND

When you're drawn to both
men and women, sex is
everywhere. So many of my
friendships are based
on attraction. It would be
restful not to be craving.
I started at age six,
and it still makes me crazy.
Happily, when I'm with someone,
I don't stray. But in my mind
I'm a hopeless sex fiend.

MAN IN THE TEA HOUSE

What must it be like
to be so good-looking?
Does he have a marvelous
sense of self? Does he
look in the mirror and see
an excellent person?
Or does seeing perfection
bore him, make him wish
for an inner flaw, something
to render him more human?
Is he human? I'd like
to speak to him,
see if words flow effortlessly
from his beautiful lips,
see if he says, I'm tired,
I'm not happy. But I
don't get the chance,
he drinks his tea and goes
leaving a wake of questions
behind his ideal manifestation.

THE SMILE

A young, good-looking, moon-faced
man tells me by his glance
I've grown old, but then
surprises me by smiling widely
and I'm twenty again.
His smile is like anyone's smile
except for the innocence behind it,
that doesn't even know it's innocent.
It "lights up the room" as they say,
and it's true, I'm happy in its glow.
Now I'm smiling too, with a smile
that can last only so long
before it fades.

WIDE-EYED

I stare helplessly
at this woman in the teahouse
with wavy red hair,
wide-spaced, large, green eyes,
high cheekbones,
porcelain skin.
I try to avoid her
but it's no use,
she's a magnet.
I don't want to embarrass her
or anger her
but my eyes just keep honing
in on her several freckles,
each one a focus
for eyes that prize beauty
in this very special form.

A LONG RELATIONSHIP

for David on the occasion of our 30th anniversary

Things just keep going on.
We've been together thirty years
and everything is fine, we're still
in love. We've had peaks and valleys
and other peaks and this current peak
is splendid. I've devoted my life to you
and you yours to me, but our relationship
has been a series of moments like this one
and more to come until the end of life.
We don't know when the end will be
but we'll keep going in love
for as long as we're here.

THE PINNACLE

The most exciting thing in life
for me is not the latest space launch,
a great new symphony,
the view of Mt. Diablo snow-capped,
but you emerging from your room
after I haven't seen you for a couple of hours,
lamb's wool hair and shining brown eyes,
for even though after thirty years
I know every crevice of your face,
every curve of your body,
nothing tops that—you,
looking and talking . . . at me!

ROMANTIC

I trudge along, my legs
heavy and slow. Davey
links arms with me, which
helps, if only mentally.
It takes us five minutes
to walk from the house to the car.
It's romantic: one old
geezer helping another.
Who would have predicted
it would come to this?
Two young men discovered
each other, high on life.
Now the only thing we're
high on is Vicodin.
We continue along,
Davey helping me to walk,
I calming him down,
each of us making it possible
for the other to live.
I reach out to thank him
for all he does.
I write a poem about
his love and mine.

OUR HOME

is small and snug.
We like to sit on
our living room couch
to watch TV.
The couch is flanked
by two chairs for guests.
Each of our bedrooms
has a bed, desk and
chair, with room to type
on our computers
and sleep the sleep
of the just. Our kitchen
has a stove and a
refrigerator and David
cooks happily there.
We live a simple life
in our simple house.

ILLNESS

THE IRON WILL

I face the future with an iron will:
the diagnosis, the illness,
the pain, the deterioration.
I will not let these defeat me.
I will look forward
to each passing day,
savor each moment,
and not waver before the End.
Without a God, I find
in myself strength to persist.
Illness, you should be ashamed
of yourself for plaguing me.
Beware! I'm stronger than you.

DIALYSIS IS FUN!

I read the paper, talk
on the phone, listen
to music, watch TV.
I don't have
to go to work,
am entertained
by the technicians,
and am taken care of.
It's just life,
more life,
more and more
for as long as possible.

DIALYSIS AND TIME

Each session of dialysis
goes a little faster
just as time goes faster
with age. And each week
goes a little faster too.
I've been in dialysis one year.
The first week seemed an eternity,
but now the months fly by
and my main thought is that
I would like dialysis
to continue forever.

TO MY UNCLE SAM

in memory of Sam Huber, 1900-1972

What can you tell me?
How to stay sharp
while almost paralyzed?
How to fill a difficult day
with painting and witticisms?
How to have the guts
to keep going? I wish
I could speak with you,
learn from you.
But you're silent, and
all I can do is copy you,
try to face what may be in store
the way you did.

SAM

developed Parkinson's
at fifty. He was head
of the art department
at Benjamin Franklin High School
in the Bronx when
a kid running in a corridor
knocked him down,
breaking his arm,
accelerating his decline.
I never knew him as a healthy man.
I do remember helping him
out of chairs or bed,
walking him to the bathroom
where he spent a lot of time.
His hands trembled as he ate
or trimmed his mustache.
I never played with him,
never walked with him in Central Park.
His illness towered over my
childhood like a shadow.

DEVELOPING PARKINSON'S?

My hands have started to shake,
and my head, too, and my lips and throat
click like a timer. I realize—
nightmare become reality—
that I may have it. I remember Mom
being "mortified" by how people
stared at Uncle Sam on the sidewalk
with his shuffling gait and trembling arms.
Now I shuffle and tremble.
There's no changing it, it's *me,*
it's me who seems to have it.
I'll try not to consider it a curse, as Mom did,
God against us, but part of life,
the hand I've been dealt.

HAVING PARKINSON'S?

I seem to have it.
I'm almost used to
the idea already.
I remember Sam,
ill, yet cheerful,
cracking jokes and continuing
to paint, letting his hand
shake on the paper
to create abstract designs.
He died at 72, of a stroke.
I'm 74, and just getting started.
Mom would have considered this
a tragedy, but I don't, quite.
It's just another step
on a long road of taking my life
as it comes. How I do it is
part of the discovery—maybe
the essence of the discovery.
I'm ready to start.

NOT HAVING PARKINSON'S

Two tests show that
I don't have it after all!
I'm happy but worried.
How explain the shaking,
the shuffling gait, the
clicking of my jaw?
The result of a drug
I've taken for twenty years?
We'll try reducing it,
maybe do more tests.
I'm swimming in a sea
of uncertainty, but at least
I don't have Parkinson's.

ANXIETY AT 6 P.M.

I think I can get through life
if I take it in little units:
prepare and eat a lamb chop,
do the dishes,
watch a movie for two hours,
listen to radio news,
take the pills in my pill case,
read some pages of a novel,
drift off to sleep
as gently as possible with,
finally,
nothing to worry about . . .
unless I have bad dreams.

INSOMNIA

There's nothing to be done,
you're in its grip,
not thinking about it
is thinking about it,
it's a grand absence,
a nullity, a hole
that can't be filled,
it goes on and on
and feels infinite,
as if it will never end,
till eventually
something happens
without fanfare,
without a sound,
without your even noticing it,
and you leave it behind
in the night
with other empty things
that have no value
and no shame.

CORONAVIRUS

We who haven't directly experienced
wars or famines or depressions
now generally face life's unfairness
for the first time,
parallel to my own situation.
We suffer as I've suffered,
so I can try to help people
with lessons I've learned:
accept things as they are,
look on the bright side,
steel oneself to pain,
remember others suffer too.
It isn't easy, but it's not
the end of the world, either,
even if it feels it is.

PANDEMIC

It's not a shooting war.
People drop, but at home
or in hospitals,
not on the street or in trenches.
The country isn't invaded
by soldiers speaking a strange language,
no local girls are being raped.
There are no sounds of explosions
at City Hall or the police station.
The enemy is only a bit of protein,
faceless, mouthless, mindless,
that attaches itself to our insides
with little protruding spikes
and wears us down till we're too sick to breathe.
This is a different kind of war,
but as in all wars it's unclear who's going to win.

PROPHECY

What if we're on the way out?
If we go, juncos and orioles
will fill windowsills with loud songs
all over the deserted cities,
and foxes, quail and moose will graze
in Yankee Stadium and in between
the slabs of suburban sidewalks.
No clouds of exhaust will
fill the air and fish in the seas
will multiply. Very gradually,
each animal will evolve
in surprising ways, and maybe
eventually some will be
as intelligent as we, or more so.
This earth is not ours. We don't own
the air, the oceans, the wind.
If we want to survive—which isn't
inevitable—we'll be serving
the earth, valuing all the creatures
and the elements, cherishing
the hills and the culverts,
respecting even the lowly virus
that only wants to thrive.

UNDER THREAT

I know a lot about disease
so this pandemic doesn't affect me
as much as it might—unless
I succumb, that is.
I'm acquainted with living
under the constant threat of death—
I lived it for a year in the eighties
when told I had the "gay disease".
Take my hand, let's stroll
together under threat,
I'll whisper comforting words.
I've lived through it, and know
you can too.

THE BRASS RING

THE BRASS RING

I've been waiting for something
all my life. I don't know
what it is. Sometimes when
I hear music swell
I feel I'm approaching it.
Maybe a certain poem I've written
sends me toward it.
It must be at the center of things,
the living core,
the point around which
everything revolves.
But I can't catch it, and I'm left
at the periphery grasping
for the brass ring,
unable to secure it in my grip.

MY FATHER'S PHILOSOPHY

My father the philosopher had a
systematic view of life, in which
everything fit. Nothing messy,
like emotion, got in the way.
Any questions were answered
neatly, if without sentiment.
My rebelliousness was countered
with anger. It took me till his death
to realize that he was a vulnerable
middle son who didn't feel his parents'
love. I evolved my own ideas, and came
to question much that my father thought.
Emotion, love, was Number One for me,
and I learned to love my father for all
he tried to be, for how he tried
to love me, and did his best all his life.

PARADISE 1

"Don't expect Paradise on earth,"
counseled my Uncle Bob years ago.
I don't. Little things are enough.
Tonight I watch the 11:00 local news
and learn how new parking meters
are breaking down in Civic Center,
Van Ness Avenue is being slightly widened,
a pet cat is missing in Antioch
and the weather tomorrow will be mild and moderate.
Every little part of life
can be considered a blessing.
The little bug making its way
across my page carries
a heap of enlightenment
on its delicate and very downy back.

PARADISE 2

We relaxed on a wooden bench by the
green-brown, tiny Loiret River
at noon munching on a baguette,
ripe Camembert, salty ham,
and a cherry clafloutis fresh from
the oven. The water rippled,
light reflected off the windows
of the ancient, ramshackle houses
along the stream, green was
shooting up everywhere,
our eyes were shining—
and they say there's no paradise on earth!

AFTER A LONG DAY

The waitress works
a long day,
comes home,
unbraids her hair,
takes a bath,
goes to bed.
So the poet creates a poem
in leisurely fashion
when each gesture is part
of a relaxing celebration of the day,
after which nothing remains but
to put his head on the pillow
and rest before sleeping.

HEATHER FARMS PARK, WALNUT CREEK, CALIFORNIA

for Pat Teschner

Sunlight makes your head bob
in and out of shadow as the breeze
riffles your hair while you taste your peach.
The blanket you recline on
is brown and the grass stretches out
in every direction, toward
other shadows, blankets,
picnickers, and the lake. I take a
mental snapshot of the scene,
a real-life Seurat. This is the most
we have—a moment caught
that then returns to a play
of light, shadow, breeze, grass and water
without end.

THAI ICED TEA

Thai iced tea fits my needs
this warm March day
when my legs feel like logs
I have trouble lifting
above the pavement. Spring
will come soon and lift spirits,
though my legs will feel no lighter.
There's no complaining, though, it
"is what it is," and spring
is preferable to winter
as I sip the chilled, sweet liquid.

DAIMO CHINESE RESTAURANT

Every face is Chinese, and every seat
is taken. Steaming plates are delivered:
pork belly with greens,
Malaysian chow fun, curry brisket.
Fish and crabs swim in tanks,
ready to give it up for our appetites.
The owner recognizes me, gives me a hug.
I'm at home here, far from Beijing
where I've never been but which
I can imagine from this crowded, noisy scene.
I come here often and celebrate
things Chinese, not my people but mine no less.

COFFEE

I miss the warm, rich, bitter
taste that gave me so many
moments of satisfaction.
It reminded me of walnut wood,
earthy loam, tasty cigars.
I drank it while lunching,
talking with friends,
teaching, after dinner,
after sex. Nothing
equaled it. Then it began
to make me throw up
and I had to quit.
If only I could still
be enveloped by its strong,
comforting arms!

MUSIC AS REDEEMER

Music is insubstantial as air.
It doesn't even exist apart from
scores or performances
live or recorded.
And yet it can transform
melancholy into joy.
There is something life-affirming
even in the darkest music.
The infinitely sad Schnittke
has often lifted me up.
Why some composers speak to me
particularly is a mystery.
Just as I like certain people, I like
duParc or Mozart, or fall in love with
Bach or Rameau just as I love David or
my friends. May they be with me
at the end, when the last strand
of meaning I might perceive
might be a melody of César Franck
that lifts me out of my bed,
right out of my body!

LOUIS SPOHR

Once the most famous composer in the world,
he's now at 893 on the hit parade.
No one listens to him anymore
except me. I spend hour after hour
with his thunderous symphonies, gleaming
violin concertos, tight string quartets.
Little known too, I commune with him
across the years and genres.
We both love to make music,
and his notes and my words vibrate in sympathy.

HEARING *THE RITE OF SPRING* FOR THE FIRST TIME

Dissonant notes from the stereo
in the summer camp lounge
with its opulent cushions,
purple tapestried walls,
and music counselor with high cheekbones
seemed an adult experiment:
the music sounded "off"
and that was wonderful.
A whole new kind of music,
unlike the Bach and Mozart
my parents taught me . . .
This was just a beginning,
would lead me eventually to
Schoenberg, Webern, Boulez,
Carter . . . but for now it was
an adventure that titillated
and intrigued this youngster
who thirsted for something
beyond the banal, for the new.

OLD

GROWING OLD

The days add up and I
grow old. I marvel
that this has happened,
even while knowing
that day was added to day.
You age only once
just as you're young only once.
Is this an opportunity to seize?
What shall I do with it?
Try to understand things better?
The world resists. I try
and try, but I just grow older
and older.

AGING

My legs buckle
as I rise from bed.
My fingers fumble
with my shirt buttons.
My hands shake
as I fry eggs.
Walking to my car,
my feet hurt.
The whole day's like this.
I'm surprised at how things are.
I'm not used to it.
No one warned me it would
be like this.

OLD

Now that I'm old
I've grown philosophical.
I'm glad for what I have:
David, my friends, poetry.
I can't expect to have
good health or money.
I'm happy some days,
sad others. I may die
one of these days
but maybe not soon.
It's been a long slog
but overall a good one.
Now that I'm old
I've grown philosophical.

PERSPECTIVE

Now that I've grown old
I find that things repeat.
A world-shattering pandemic
is a repeat of 1918's.
An Afghan war is another war,
not so unusual.
A recession is one of many.
And in personal lives
changes aren't surprising:
people have been falling
in and out of love
by the millions for centuries.
The older I get,
the less original things seem.
Hopefully, by the time I die,
death also will seem familiar.

ROLLING LOGS

The days flow by
like logs on a river,
rolling gently yet
carrying lethal force,
proceeding downstream
with no particular motive
but to proceed in only one direction,
no end in sight
but the sea which waits,
bellowing,
at river's end.

THE CANYON

Now that I'm old
the canyon yawns in front of me.
Each scrub tree on its edge
and each cloud trailing above
takes its own unforgettable form.
Dust rises from the desert floor
and rocks gleam gold vermilion.
I approach the rim,
then recoil, thinking still to savor
each distinct pebble at my feet,
each clump of grass.
It's been a long trek here,
but I'm alive among the cacti
and tumbleweed, counting
each minute.
Looking back, the plain seems
unbelievable. I have come this far,
so why not proceed?
The canyon yawns deeply
and I survey its broad expanse
before taking the plunge.

SUNNY DAY

Time passes . . .
I'm still alive . . .
Am I surprised I've made it this far?
Fourteen of my friends
have died: Geoffrey, Tim, Ruth, Colin,
Sandy, John, Patric, Luther, Douglas,
Leno, Fred, Dan, Mitch, Arnold—
all unlucky compared with me.
There must be some explanation,
but if there is I can't make it out.
I carry on, embracing the living
while honoring the dead.
I throw my arms around the brethren
who still share with me the sun and moon,
who continue the trek
through the thicket of earth
to live another day,
sunny, with light and air
the natural state of things . . .

THE STOICS

lived and died courageously
without a God.
Their philosophy
was to be clear-eyed,
to face things as they are.
To think
instead of fearing.
I'd like to face the End
like them. Seneca,
Marcus Aurelius,
lend me some of your courage,
may I live and die like you!

THE OWL AND THE MOUSE

The owl swooped down
and clutched the mouse,
a simple act of gluttony
concluded by a meal.
The mouse never prayed
for its life, it lost out
as many things do,
without a thought or doubt,
yielding to a stronger philosophy
of beak and claw,
more powerful than any belief in God
or other spiritual faith.

EVERYONE DIES DIFFERENTLY

My friend Ruth declined for months
with little pain and simply slipped
away while lying on her sleeping bag
in her sunny den. Terry's dad
fought tooth and nail every second.
My father went suddenly, in his sleep.
My mother was afraid and anguished,
reaching out to hug me while she
cried out "It's so hard, it's so hard!"
David's friend went into a bedroom
at a party and was found lying in bed.
Goethe cried out "More light, more light!"
Daniel Pearl was beheaded;
what did that feel like?
Stephen woke up from a coma,
panicky, and then was gone.
My Uncle Sam died of Parkinson's,
thinking all the nurses were trying to kill him.
And there was Jesus, of course.
I wonder what mine will be like?

THE ANGEL OF DEATH

As the Angel of Death
hovers over us all
in this pandemic,
I seek a way to
defeat it. It threatens
but I kick back,
won't be bullied by Fate.
I will cherish things like
ginger apple green tea,
the Oakland A's,
or my love's perfect nose.
There are things like these
superior to death,
I collect them
like rare butterflies
that fly about looking
beautiful even though
one day they will die.
I collect and collect,
and will not stop
until the Angel finally descends.

MASKS OF TRAGEDY

When terrifying masks of tragedy
assail the soul, there's no escaping them,
and when one of them begins
to speak it shrieks like a bat
or screeches like a rusty hinge.
Horror is the name of the
slow process that plays out
against a background of blackness
and blood. Try to escape
and you're just more trapped
by the sticky glue
that holds the masks together.
Try to fly, and you're bound to the ground
in a dream of confinement and decay.
I raise my voice against this farce
but it's no use, a person is powerless
in such a landscape,
and the self's an apparition
soon dissolved into the
miasma of despair.

STREAM OF WORDS

WHISPERING

The wind whispered in the trees.
I had been tired a long time
so I lay down among the leaves.
They were soft and I slept.
I felt part of the earth,
neither dead nor alive.
My dreams reached the skies,
but my body remained on the ground.
Did I sleep a long time?
I don't know, but when I woke
everything was fresh,
glistening and clear.
The wind was whispering in the trees
but now it held a message I understood.

RACING TIME

I'd like this evening
to pass slowly, fully.
I listen to a bit of
Boccherini but it's
over before I know it.
Then I watch a movie
that's so enjoyable
the hour and a half
goes fast. I read
in bed but the pages
turn like seconds.
If only I could get
the minutes to slow down!
But then it's morning
and I'm another day
closer to the End.

PASSION

Many of us like
what we're doing,
whether running a mile
or completing a novel.
There are lots of things
to do, no one should
complain about boredom
like I used to as a kid.
I learned that
if you put yourself
into something it
will turn interesting.
Poker, cars, birds,
weather, golf, math—
it doesn't matter,
anything will do.
For me it's poetry,
that quirky, obscure,
poignant way of
showing an interest in life—
throwing yourself
into things
with joy and passion.

STREAM OF WORDS

Words buckle up willy nilly
in this sentence like boulders
in a creek, impeding the flow
of my thoughts, making ideas bunch
like floating leaves, driving
minnows into narrow passageways
which they barely escape
until my bare foot stubs itself
on sharp mica and bleeds
into the muddy, cloudy mix.
I want this stream to flow
effortlessly, for my words
to be liquid without barriers,
verse that's easy, smooth
and painless.

BLUE JEANS

seem like a good subject
for a poem. They could symbolize
solid, everyday labor,
pants to work comfortably in.
Let's talk about all the tasks
we could work together, reader—
you reading comfortably,
me sweating out the symbolism,
We could continue until we're done,
then take off the jeans
and end the poem.

THE APPLE TREE

in the back yard
is gnarly and twisted.
It sprouts new leaves each spring
as if it were a teenager again,
my age when I planted it
hoping for eventual fruit.
It provided apples reliably,
but now is too old.
Its lessons, though, are as green
as ever. I don't produce fruit
now either, just poems.

LIBRARIAN

It's a cliché: spectacles
on a chain, old age,
shushing index finger.
Or I: introvert,
academic bent,
dreams to fulfill.
My dream was to write poetry.
I arranged books,
cataloged, answered
questions. It was
the perfect day job.
Did I achieve anything major?
No, I just did my work,
came home,
ate dinner,
and then dove in,
typing to 2 AM
until my dream of that day
was fulfilled.
Daytime I was a librarian,
nighttime a poet,
and they fit together well.

READING RILKE FOR THE FIRST TIME

Bored, unfulfilled, I wandered
campus looking, searching,
into the college library,
into the college bookstore,
where I came upon an orange-
and-green paperback titled
Duino Elegies and something
told me to buy it, some voice,
some spiritual power. I took it
to the banks of the Crum River
where I read "Who, if I cried,
would hear me among the angelic orders?"
I read and read until I'd finished.
Boredom and emptiness
were forgotten and it seemed
life had a purpose, which was
this afternoon, this sitting
by the Crum reading magic words
over and over, like a
magic spell, like an answer.

READING ROBBE-GRILLET IN PARIS

Summer sun blanched the pages
a brilliant white as I sat
on a wrought iron chair
in the Luxembourg Gardens
where kids floated boats in the reflecting pool
and lovers strolled hand-in-hand.
My underlining was in a scholarly black
that contrasted with the brilliance of the day.
The subject was the *nouveau roman*
and the author Robbe-Grillet,
advocating a new kind of fiction
without characters or plot.
I was to read and then analyze
for college back home.
The boldness of the ideas
mingled with the whiteness of the pages
and the brilliant light,
the characteristic light of Paris
on a summer day.

THE ROMANCE

Sometimes, when you don't
have a life, write a poem.
Make up a grand romance,
a fine friendship
or a tragic death.
It can be believable,
for life is full of surprises.
Imagine a lover with whom
you'll share your life,
kiss her until there are
no kisses left. Make her
the summit of all your hopes,
and wish she'll outlive you.
There is only one true story,
of which this is just one example.
I love her, I love her,
and that's the summary
of my made-up tale.

REVOLUTION

REVOLUTION

Several people objected
and others joined in
until there was a torrent
of dissent. Some were
rebelling against their fathers,
others protested because
they were poor, and still others
hated the idea of God.
They built barricades,
threw stones at the police,
tossed Molotov cocktails.
They wanted a better world.
But the police used bullets,
the ministry of justice jailed opponents,
the leaders of the insurrection were executed,
and the revolution was put off
for quite a few years.

WORLD WAR

There have been more than two
of them, but lacking the name.
Not *all* the countries in the world
fought in 1916 and 1941,
and many nations of Europe
were involved in the Hundred Years' War.
War is war. It doesn't matter whether
swords or guns or bombs are used,
there's always blood. Blood:
the universal of human society,
the *lingua franca,* the Esperanto.
It's been flowing for millennia
and shows no sign of stopping.

TWENTY SOLDIERS

Twenty of them marched
in unison down the avenue.
It was wartime
and it was freezing,
but that didn't bother them,
for they held to a single thought—
the killing they hoped to do—
and nothing could dissuade them.
They possessed a faith
stronger than a belief in God.
Nothing could affect them
except a bullet in the gut,
which was a battlefield
and four hours away,
and they weren't afraid of anything
yet.

CIVIL WAR

There were two sides.
(There are always at least two sides.)
They hated each other
for the color of their teeth,
for the curve of their upper arms,
for the furrows in their brows,
and even for the hue of one leader's skin.
They spoke against each other's ideas
and despised one another's laughs and tears.
Yet they shared a common heritage.
(No one fights like brothers.)
They even quarreled over how to manage
disease. A demagogue
galvanized one side more than ever
leading up to a crucial election.
Will there be another civil war?

RODENTS UNITED

Groundhogs and woodchucks
gathered round for a colloquy
of rodents who chose to supplant
humans as the dominant race.
One spoke up for war
against the "pink and brown ones,"
another advocated non-violent
action, a third called for overwhelming
the world with great numbers.
But the humans responded
with jets, bombs and tanks
and the animals lost
for the millionth time.

CAMPAIGN

Escaping to Canada would be one way
of avoiding the agony of this
Presidential campaign.
That country has a liberal leader
and socialized medicine.
It has a lot of rain, though,
and a bitter winter.
Our bright American spring sun
bakes the pate of our leader,
so he can barely think—
if you could call what he does thinking.
Our opposition candidates flail
this way and that,
hurting each other.
What will happen?
The sun shines down
warming us all
with the illusion of summer
before autumn comes
and the election brings
catastrophe—or hope.

THEY

They spoke several languages
and were tolerant
of diverse philosophies.
There were many of them
and they gained a lot of power.
Nothing was as it had been.
The world was infused with compassion
and dialogue became the norm.
Spirituality was at a peak.
But they were mortal
and started to die off,
and who could say
whether spirit or death had triumphed?

THE IVORY TOWER

When I was young my family
and people around me
saw the university as the place
of Truth, where
people who *knew* assembled,
people who were acquainted
with history, philosophy and science
and knew what life was about and for.
They wouldn't have admitted it,
but they felt superior to janitors,
nurses, policemen and bus drivers,
not to mention rock 'n' roll singers
and jazz pianists. Naturally,
I adopted the same outlook.
But over time I've learned a lot about
how most people contribute
to society—how firemen save more lives
than professors, how a longshoreman
can know as much as a philosopher,
how a swami is more serene than a theologian,
how a middle school teacher can be smarter
than a political scientist.
I know more now than I used to. The ivory tower
is just one place of Truth among many.
I'm done thinking myself superior.

HOT AND COLD

HOT

It was scalding hot.
Sweat poured off my skin
like soup off a saucepan.
It was summer,
awaited for so long
but now too sultry,
causing suffering and death.
Mouse carcasses littered
the garden and sparrow bones
mixed with them.
The heat was intolerable but,
having wished for it,
I couldn't find it undesirable.
I wanted cool, though:
an ice cube across my lips,
cool spray on my torso.
No cold could be too cold.

COLD

It's freezing cold.
My hands are numb,
my fingers stiff.
I've been on this trek
for centuries now,
stretching out the years
as time slows down.
I am a creature of winter,
where death rules
over every branch and twig.
I've almost reached my goal now,
the point at which life
faces death and the minutes stop.
I will morph into a statue of ice,
human form in death's dominion.

NORTHERN CALIFORNIA WEATHER

Here you can't complain:
the air's temperate year-round.
None of the burning heat of Los Angeles
or icy cold of East Coast winters.
Just so, in between hot and cold
most of the year—the climate
rarely causes you to suffer.
All suffering is for other reasons,
and is lessened by the balmy air.
Life, our climate tells us, is a
pleasant undertaking,
an occasion for celebration.

ROARING

The roar of a thousand lions
filled the arena. They
wouldn't stop, there was
no controlling them,
pandemonium was the
order of the day.
I tried to distinguish my voice
from the cacophony but it
got lost. Oh lions,
let me be human, let me
be an individual free of your
communal, powerful dissonance!

WINTER ON THE EAST COAST

Snow and ice pile up
by the curb as the sun fades
and the air chills, freezes.
Ah winter! exclaims the poet
unaccustomed to it all,
having lived all these years
in California and lost
the old life in the East.
A brief stay is all it takes
for it all to come back--
fingers freezing, cheeks numb--
and he lives it all again,
the feeling of no feeling,
the loss of warmth until loss
is all he has left.

SMOKING

Cigarette smoke from the car
in front of me reaches
my nostrils with its acrid yet
captivating smell, reminding me
of veal dinners in Orléans,
puffs sandwiched between courses
filling my lungs with warmth,
giving me energy, satisfying me
as nothing else could.
Now it's a pleasure that lasts
a moment, no guilt because
involuntary, not that harmful
because brief, proof that happiness
might be an accident, with no guarantees.

WAITING

At the Japanese restaurant
I order California rolls to go.
Dialysis is in three hours.
I'm waiting, but I don't know
for what. For the four hours
of tedium? For the rolls,
which I'll enjoy? For something
to happen which I can't predict?
I've waited all my life
for something tangible
but waiting seems futile now.
I'm ready to go after it
if the right time comes.

THE EMPTY HOUSE

The house is empty,
and has been for years.
A decade ago it was built
and freshly painted.
But windows were never put in.
Two cars, the same two cars,
are always parked in the driveway.
We drive past every day,
and nothing ever changes.
Who built it? Why
don't they live there?
What will happen to it?
The house is reliable—a constant
reminder that life is enigmatic.

IGNORANCE

This afternoon I read about the ancient movement
of Zoroastrians from Persia to India
for which historians have no clear explanation.
I then turned on the TV to encounter
a rap singer I'd never heard of.
A friend called and told me
he can't land a job and doesn't know why--
he has all the qualifications.
The evening paper tried to describe
the Russian oil industry,
how no one knows who really has the power.
I ate a simple dinner
only to hear on the radio of a traffic jam on Highway 80
caused by no particular accident.
Finally I put my head on my pillow
but had trouble sleeping
for reasons I don't really understand.

TROUBADOUR SONG

TROUBADOUR SONG

I freeze, I burn.
I can't have what I want.
Your lovely voice
rips my heart apart.
I've loved you years
and known little
but your lips.
It is not your fault.
It is not my fault.
Fate separates us.
I will never touch those lips again.
It's no one's fault.
I freeze, I burn.

BODY, HEART, IMAGINATION

Feet are meant to step,
hands to grasp. I trudge along,
feet heavy as weights, and
drop things after picking them up.
But my brain and heart
are active as ever, filled
with desire for your sweet mouth,
your lips and tongue, making
me feel almost normal
even though our kisses
take place only in my imagination.

VIVACIOUSNESS

is the quality I most
prize in a woman,
and you have it.
"Full of life and spirits,"
the dictionary says:
you speak with excitement,
humor, musicality, sweetness.
Just listening to you raises
my spirits without my having
to do anything. Just being
around you makes me
feel full of life. From *vivere,*
"*to live,*" you are the very
essence of life for me,
the definition of being here.

YOUR NOSE

Your nose is perfect.
It doesn't fall into any category:
broad, hook, snub, aquiline.
It isn't large
and it isn't small.
I've never seen one like it.
I love to gaze at it,
continually surprised
that a nose could be so shapely.
To reach over and kiss it
would be my dream, but
that might startle you.
I stare and blink and marvel
that a simple nose
could be so charming.
But it makes its own way in the world
and I imagine it's trodden a path
among athletes and intellectuals
and artists that's left them speechless,
so matchless is it.

YOUR FACE

How describe it?
Its wide mouth
reveals dimples
and little even teeth
when you smile
your pixyish grin,
lips that know how to give
such great pleasure,
cap of smooth brown hair,
straight, perfectly shaped nose,
and hazel eyes, oh those eyes!,
that shine with warmth
at one lucky enough
to be in their line of sight.

GLEAMING

My nerve endings are alert
and I can tell
my eyes are gleaming.
Or maybe it's that
your eyes are gleaming
in me, filling up
my brain and body
like some inland sun
warming the interior.
What is happening?
I notice a tree limb
by my window
I hadn't seen before.
My belly keeps jumping into my throat.
This just kind of happened
without intention or plan.
Who could have predicted it?

AWAY FROM YOU

The days inch along
as your face shines in memory.
Ahead of me, it is a blossom
promising to open.
I wait, hands ready,
to touch sweet-smelling petals.
I will wait as long as necessary
for the bloom to meet my lips
and dissolve into a nectar of bliss.

ONE HUNDRED FINCHES

Your dove's heart brings me peace.
Your laughter allows me to breathe.
Your voice is a hundred finches singing.
Your breasts are the obsessions
of my dreamlife.
My memory thrills at the thought of your lips.
You give me brilliant mornings
plus glittery evenings before sleep.
You bring, each day, the hope
that I will soon see you again.

MY HOLLYWOOD

I watch Jane Fonda in *Klute*
and all I can think of is
your breasts, your lips,
your skin.
I watch Grace Kelly in
"Dial M for Murder"
and all I want is to hold her
as I'd hold you,
vulnerable and sweet.
Every movie kiss reminds me
of you and makes me want to kiss you.
There's only one female star in the world
for me,
and that's you.

OTHER LIFE

In another life I think
we might have been man and wife.
You have the intellect of a philosopher,
a voice that charms,
and your vivacious personality
makes life more exciting.
But in this life we are best friends,
sharing poetry, music and Nature
while beneath the surface
some deep current is flowing
that may never reach the surface.

NOTES

"I Am Bisexual": *The Charterhouse of Parma,* novel by Stendhal.

"I Am Who I Am": Silver Lake is in the Pinnacles Peaks in the Sierra Mountains of California.

"People Label Me": Thousand Islands Lakes is in the Pinnacles.

"The Pinnacles": Mount Diablo is in Contra Costa County, California.

"Coronavirus": Global pandemic that began in early 2020.

"Paradise 1": Civic Center and Van Ness Avenue are in San Francisco.

"Paradise 2": The Loiret River is in the Loiret region of France; it is a tributary of the Loire River.

"Daimo Chinese Restaurant": In Richmond, California.

"Louis Spohr": German composer 1784-1859.

"The Stoics": Seneca and Marcus Aurelius, Roman Stoic philosophers.

"The Angel of Death": 2020 Coronavirus pandemic.

"Reading Rilke for the First Time": Rainier Maria Rilke, *Duino Elegies.*

"Reading Robbe-Grillet in Paris": Alain Robbe-Grillet, French novelist.

"Campaign": U.S. Presidential campaign of 2020

"Smoking": Orléans, city in north central France.

ABOUT THE AUTHOR

Marc Elihu Hofstadter was born in New York City in 1945. He received his B.A. in French Literature from Swarthmore College in 1967 and his Ph.D. in Literature from the University of California at Santa Cruz in 1975. He has taught American literature at Santa Cruz, the Université d'Orléans (on a Fulbright Lectureship) and Tel Aviv University. In 1980 he received his Master's degree in Library and Information Studies from the University of California at Berkeley and, from 1982 to 2005, served as the Librarian of the City and County of San Francisco's transit agency, the San Francisco Municipal Railway. He has published eight previous volumes of poetry—*House of Peace* (Mother's Hen Press), *Visions* (Scarlet Tanager Press), *Shark's Tooth* (Regent Press), *Luck* (Scarlet Tanager Press), *Rising at 5 AM* (Latitude Press), *Memories I've Forgotten* (Dog Ear Publishing), *Autumnal* (self-published) and *Life Is Its Own Meaning* (self-published)—and a volume of essays entitled *Healing the Split: The Collected Essays of Marc Elihu Hofstadter* (Dog Ear Publishing), all of which are available on amazon.com. His poems, essays and translations of French poems have appeared in over sixty magazines. Hofstadter is a member of one of the United States' leading intellectual families. His uncle Robert Hofstadter won the Nobel Prize in physics, his cousins Douglas and Richard Hofstadter were both awarded the Pulitzer Prize, his father was a professor of philosophy at Columbia University and three other universities, his mother Manya Huber an award-winning concert pianist, and his uncle Samuel Huber a noted painter. Hofstadter lives in the retirement community of Rossmoor in Walnut Creek, California with his partner of many years, the paper doll artist David Zurlin.

Printed in Great Britain
by Amazon